DATE DUE

FEB 1 0 1997			
JUL 1 7 1997			
AUG 1 1 1997			

Cornerstones of Freedom

The Assassination of Martin Luther King Jr.

R. Conrad Stein

CHILDREN'S PRESS®
A Division of Grolier Publishing
New York • London • Hong Kong • Sydney
Danbury, Connecticut

Library of Congress Cataloging-in-Publication Data

Stein, R. Conrad.
   The assassination of Martin Luther King Jr. / by R. Conrad Stein.
      p. cm. — (Cornerstones of freedom)
   Includes index.
   Summary: Chronicles the events leading up to, and the immediate
aftermath of, the murder of one of the best-known figures in the
United States civil rights movement.
   ISBN: 0-516-20004-6
   1. King, Martin Luther, Jr., 1929–1968—Assassination—Juvenile
literature. [1. King, Martin Luther, Jr., 1929–1968—Assassination.
2. Civil rights workers. 3. Afro-Americans—Biography.] I. Title.
II. Series.
E185.97.K5S75 1996
364.1′524′092—dc20
                                                                96-2018
                                                                   CIP
                                                                   AC

A dismal rain fell on Memphis, Tennessee, on January 31, 1968. The storm was so intense that city authorities feared it would interfere with garbage collection. To save money that day, officials sent their African-American garbage collectors home. (At the time, city workers were segregated.) On payday, the blacks received only two hours of wages for the rainy day while the white crews were paid for working the entire day. Reduced wages was only one of many grievances that the black employees had against the leaders in the Memphis city government. Finally, after several years of unfair treatment, the Memphis African-American sanitation workers went on strike. They called upon Dr. Martin Luther King Jr. to support them and their cause.

Memphis sanitation workers strike as National Guard troops look on.

Martin Luther King Jr. grew up in the segregated South. He was forced to attend all-black schools. He was even unable to drink from water fountains labeled WHITES ONLY. Despite the restrictions limiting his life, he became an ordained minister and earned a doctor's degree in theology. His formal title was Reverend Dr. Martin Luther King Jr., but some of his close friends called him "Doc."

In 1955, King led a boycott against the Montgomery, Alabama, bus system. The purpose of the boycott was to protest segregation

Segregated drinking fountains

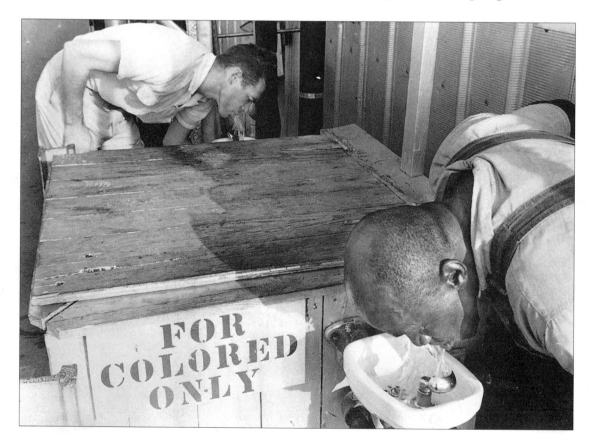

on the city's public buses. Beginning with that protest, King became the guiding force behind the drive to break down the barriers of racial segregation in the United States. He delivered powerful speeches about equality for all people. In 1963, he spoke before a quarter of a million people gathered at the Lincoln Memorial in Washington, D.C.: "I have a dream that my four little children will one day live in a nation where they will be judged not by the color of their skin, but by the content of their character." As the crowd roared its approval, King repeated again and again, "I have a dream. I have a dream today!"

Martin Luther King Jr. addresses the crowd at the Lincoln Memorial during the 1963 march on Washington.

King based his civil rights crusade on the power of nonviolent protest. He and his followers sometimes marched through neighborhoods where they were pelted with stones, yet he told the marchers not to strike back. "Violence is self-defeating," he said. He urged fighting "with the weapon of love." His belief in nonviolence won him praise around the world and earned him the Nobel Peace Prize in 1964.

Accepting the 1964 Nobel Peace Prize

When King arrived in Memphis in 1968, the civil rights movement faced a crucial turning point. Many African-Americans were dissatisfied with the slow progress that nonviolent protest was making. Some of them chanted the cry, "Black Power!" This often implied black supremacy, or an overthrow of white society. King was opposed to this idea. Also, by the spring of 1968, the United States was gripped by violence. Race riots had flared in several cities. The United States military was involved in the war in Vietnam, which King opposed. College campuses rocked with angry demonstrations. King called the turmoil and the divisions in the country, "a virus of hate [that] if unchecked will lead inevitably to our moral and spiritual doom."

This demonstration against the war in Vietnam took place in New York City in 1967.

On April 3, 1968, King spoke in front of two thousand supporters of the Memphis sanitation workers' strike. He decided to attend the rally only at the last minute and had to address the crowd without prepared notes. "Like anybody I would like to live a long life," he said. "Longevity has its place. But I'm not concerned about that now. I just want to do God's will. And He's allowed me to go up to the mountain." His voice grew louder and more intense. "And I've looked over, and I've seen the promised land. I may not get there with you, but I want you to know tonight that we as a people will get to the promised land. So I'm happy tonight. I'm not worried about anything. I'm not fearing any man. Mine eyes have seen the glory of the coming of the Lord."

The crowd exploded in cheers and applause. King's message was inspiring and uplifting. But many of those present feared the words came from a man contemplating his own death. King

King addressed the strikers the day before his death.

had dedicated his life to overcoming prejudice. The threat of death haunted him ever since he had become the nation's foremost civil rights leader. In 1958, he was stabbed by a black woman named Izola Curry in New York City. The knife narrowly missed his heart. Even his recent flight to Memphis was delayed because someone had called the airline and claimed to have put a bomb on board his plane. And at the moment he spoke before the crowd assembled in Memphis, no one could have known that it was the last speech he would ever make.

In 1958, Izola Curry was arrested after she stabbed Martin Luther King Jr.

The next day, April 4, 1968, James Earl Ray registered at Mrs. Brewer's rooming house on South Main Street in Memphis. Stuffed in his suitcase was a Memphis newspaper with a front-page photo of King entering room 306 at the Lorraine Motel. Ray, a thirty-nine-year-old white man, requested a room at the back of the rooming house. He seemed pleased when he discovered his bathroom window offered a clear view of the Lorraine Motel and room 306, which was less than 200 yards (183 m) away.

Mrs. Brewer's rooming house, where James Earl Ray rented a room on April 4, 1968

King (second from right) on the balcony of his motel room with aides (from left) Hosea Williams, the Rev. Jesse Jackson, and Ralph Abernathy.

At about 6:00 P.M. on April 4, Dr. Martin Luther King Jr. stepped onto the balcony outside his room. He had a busy evening planned—dinner at a friend's house and then a mass meeting at the Mason Street Temple. Below the balcony stood Ben Branch, who was slated to sing at the meeting. King called down to him to sing the song, "Precious Lord, Take My Hand." He called out, "Sing it real pretty, Ben." A minute later a shot rang out. Some witnesses said it sounded like a firecracker. Ralph Abernathy, King's friend and fellow minister, saw King fall to the balcony floor and rushed to his side. When Abernathy saw King lying motionless he said, "Oh, my God." From down below, a woman screamed.

Horror, panic, and confusion swept the motel grounds. Police raced to the scene. An ambulance siren wailed in the distance. In Mrs. Brewer's rooming house, James Earl Ray charged past another guest in the second floor hallway and rushed down the back stairs. Witnesses later said he dropped a long bundle or package in front of a store, jumped into a white Mustang with Alabama license plates, and sped away. Police retrieved the package and discovered it contained a rifle with a telescopic sight.

Witnesses point in the direction of the gunshots as King lies bleeding on the balcony.

An ambulance speeds King to the hospital.

View of the Lorraine Motel from Mrs. Brewer's rooming house (King's room is circled)

At 7:05 P.M., doctors at St. Joseph's Hospital in Memphis officially pronounced Martin Luther King Jr. dead. A single bullet had severed his spinal cord, killing him almost instantly. Around the country, radio and television stations interrupted their regular programs to announce King's death. Some people were glad to hear about King's death because they thought of him as a troublemaker. But the overwhelming majority of citizens agreed with the statement issued later by President Lyndon Johnson, "America is shocked and saddened by the brutal slaying."

In the King home in Atlanta, Georgia, Coretta Scott King received a telephone call from her husband's young assistant, Jesse Jackson. "Coretta," he said. "Doc just got shot." Mrs. King had always worried about her husband's safety. Jackson had not yet said whether Martin was dead, but Coretta immediately sensed that the world would never be the same for her and her four children. She later wrote, "It [the news] hit me hard—not surprise, but shock—that the call I seemed subconsciously to be waiting for all our lives had come."

With the death of King, the nation lost a civil rights leader, but the King family lost a husband and father, as well.

Many African-Americans greeted the word of King's death with outrage. Rumors spread in some black communities that he was gunned down by United States government agents. In Washington, D.C., an influential Black Power leader, Stokely Carmichael, exclaimed, "When white America killed Dr. King last night, she declared war on us." Riots broke out in 168 cities and towns throughout the country. Angry mobs looted stores and torched buildings. Fires consumed Chicago's West Side and smoke billowed above the neighborhoods.

In many cities, angry mobs rioted and looted stores in response to King's death.

The worst rioting erupted in Washington, D.C. Ten people were killed in the capital. Arsonists started more than seven hundred fires. Some of the blazes burned only a few blocks away from the White House. The smell of smoke filled the air and the sidewalks were covered with broken glass. National Guard troops were called in to protect the White House and the Capitol building. Many Washingtonians who lived through that time will never forget the sight of machine guns set up on Pennsylvania Avenue.

National Guard troops protect the Capitol building during the days of rioting that occurred following King's death.

Rioting destroyed this block in Los Angeles.

Across the nation, the rioting lasted for three days and nights. Forty-six people were killed. Some victims died in the crossfire between police and looters. Before the riots subsided, there was $45 million worth of property damage. Army troops patrolled Chicago, Washington, D.C., and Baltimore.

Though the unrest was widespread, most African-Americans remained peaceful. In fact, many noted with bitterness that innocent people were being killed, injured, and burned out of their homes all in the name of Martin Luther King Jr., a man devoted to peace. Coretta Scott King later wrote, "Though I fully understood the desperate frustration with which the rioters reacted to Martin's death, it seemed an ironic tribute to the apostle of nonviolence."

Immediately after the killing, Mrs. King faced the painful task of telling her children they would never see their father again. It was most difficult to explain to the youngest member of the family. Five-year-old Bernice had not yet been told of her father's death when the family went to the Atlanta airport to meet the casket. In her book *My Life with Martin Luther King, Jr.,*

Mrs. King recalled, "[Bernice] started looking around and she asked, 'Mommy, where's Daddy?' I was silent and she said again, 'Mommy, where is Daddy?' By this time my heart was breaking. Finally I took her in my arms and sat down with her, and I said, 'Bunny, Daddy is lying down in his casket in the back of the plane, and he is asleep. When you see him, he won't be able to speak to you.' I could not explain any more to her. . . ."

King, with his daughter, Bernice

King's body was flown from Memphis to Atlanta for his funeral.

The funeral service for Dr. Martin Luther King Jr. was held on April 9, 1968, at the Ebenezer Baptist Church in Atlanta. It was the same church where King's father and grandfather had preached. Twenty-three United States senators, forty-seven congressmen, and three governors attended the funeral. Jacqueline Kennedy, widow of slain President John F. Kennedy, was there. Also present was Robert Kennedy, the brother of

the president. At the time, Robert Kennedy was a popular choice to become president himself. But two months after King's murder, Robert Kennedy was also killed by an assassin.

Coretta Scott King during the funeral service

Inside the church the mourners listened to a sermon King had delivered just two months earlier: "If any of you are around when I have to meet my day, I don't want a long funeral. And if you get somebody to deliver the eulogy, tell him not to talk too long. . . . I'd like someone to mention that day that Martin Luther King Jr. tried to give his life serving others. I'd like for someone to say that Martin Luther King Jr. tried to love somebody. . . ."

After the service a funeral march began that led to the South View Cemetery where King was to be buried. An estimated 150,000 people joined the procession. More than 120 million viewers watched on television. The casket bearing King's body was carried on a farm cart drawn by two mules. The mule wagon was a symbol of the Poor People's Campaign that King was planning to launch. He had hoped to lead a great congregation of blacks and whites—united by poverty—on a march through Washington, D.C., to demand justice for the nation's poor. Finally, the funeral procession reached the cemetery. The gospel singer Mahalia Jackson sang "Precious Lord, Take My Hand," the song King requested moments before he was shot.

King's family walked behind the mule cart.

In the weeks following the shooting, James Earl Ray loomed as the prime suspect. Police identified him largely through fingerprints he left at the rooming house. Tracking him down, however, proved difficult. He had registered at Mrs. Brewer's rooming house under the name John L. Millard. Ray was accustomed to using false names. Other names he used were Eric Starvo Galt, Harvey Lowmiller, and John Willard. He had spent much of his adult life on the run from the law.

Ray grew up an impoverished farm boy in Missouri. His criminal career began at a young

James Earl Ray in 1960

age and he was often in and out of jail. In 1960, Ray attempted to rob a supermarket. He was caught and sentenced to twenty years in prison.

While behind bars, Ray became a jailhouse lawyer. He advised other inmates on how they could reverse their convictions in court. On April 23, 1967, Ray escaped from the Jefferson City Prison in Missouri by hiding in a bread truck as it left the grounds. Outside prison walls, Ray drifted to California, Mexico, and Canada. His path finally led to Memphis, Tennessee, and to Dr. Martin Luther King Jr.

On June 8, 1968, a little more than two months after King's murder, James Earl Ray was arrested at Heathrow Airport in London, England. He was brought back to the United States under heavy guard. At his trial he astonished the country by pleading guilty to the crime and claiming he was the sole assassin. He was sentenced to ninety-nine years in prison.

Ray's shocking admission of guilt left two important questions unanswered: First, why did Ray kill King? Second, did he really act alone? At an early age, Ray developed a hatred for blacks. Inmates who knew him in prison claimed he spoke bitterly against Martin Luther King Jr. Yet was this general hatred toward blacks a powerful-enough motive for him to murder someone he had never met? Many Americans believe Ray was paid by someone else to be the sniper.

Ray continues to serve his ninety-nine year sentence.

When speaking to police and to court authorities, Ray denied there was any group behind the assassination. But soon after his trial he recanted his confession. He said the real murderer was a man named Raoul. But Ray's descriptions of Raoul were vague, and detectives believed that Raoul was another made-up character. Although the case against Ray was closed long ago, many doubts and questions remain.

After his death, Martin Luther King Jr. was praised and honored even more graciously than he was during his life. Few Americans have possessed his eloquence or his single-minded dedication to peaceful change in the United States. King's birthday, celebrated each year on the third Monday in January, became a federal holiday in 1983. Throngs of people regularly visit his grave in Atlanta, Georgia. Carved into his tombstone are the words he used to end his 1963 "I Have a Dream" speech: "Free at last, free at last, thank God Almighty, I'm free at last."

King's birthday became a federal holiday in 1983.

"I HAVE A DREAM"

Following are excerpts from the famous speech given by Martin Luther King Jr. on August 28, 1963, at the Lincoln Memorial in Washington, D.C.:

I say to you today, my friends, so even though we face the difficulties of today and tomorrow, I still have a dream. It is a dream deeply rooted in the American dream.

I have a dream that one day this nation will rise up and live out the true meaning of its creed: "We hold these truths to be self-evident; that all men are created equal." I have a dream that one day on the red hills of Georgia the sons of former slaves and the sons of former slaveowners will be able to sit down together at the table of brotherhood.

I have a dream that my four little children will one day live in a nation where they will not be judged by the color of their skin but by the content of their character.

This is our hope. This is the faith that I go back to the South with. With this faith we will be able to hew out of the mountain of despair a stone of hope. With this faith we will be able to transform the jangling discords of our nation into a beautiful symphony of brotherhood.

With this faith we will be able to work together, to pray together, to struggle together, to go to jail together, to stand up for freedom together, knowing that we will be free one day.

And this will be the day. This will be the day when all of God's children will be able to sing with new meaning, "My country 'tis of thee, sweet land of liberty, of thee I sing. Land where my fathers died, land of the Pilgrims' pride, from every mountainside, let freedom ring."

And if America is to be a great nation, this must become true. So let freedom ring from the prodigious hilltops of New Hampshire. Let freedom ring from the mighty mountains of New York. Let freedom ring from the heightening Alleghenies of Pennsylvania!

Let freedom ring from the snowcapped Rockies of Colorado! Let freedom ring from the curvaceous slopes of California! But not only that; let freedom ring from Stone Mountain of Georgia! Let freedom ring from Lookout Mountain of Tennessee! Let freedom ring from every hill and every molehill of Mississippi. From every mountainside, let freedom ring.

And when this happens, and when we allow freedom to ring, when we let it ring from every village and every hamlet, from every state and every city, we will be able to speed up that day when all of God's children, black men and white men, Jews and Gentiles, Protestants and Catholics, will be able to join hands and sing in the words of the old Negro spiritual, "Free at last! Free at last! Thank God Almighty, we are free at last!"

Each year hundreds of visitors pay their respects at the gravesite of Martin Luther King Jr. in Atlanta, Georgia. This memorial provides an enduring reminder of King's importance to the civil rights movement.

GLOSSARY

apostle – person with important beliefs; supporter

assassin – person who commits murder

boycott – refusal to buy or use a product in order to protest policies
of the producer

crusade – project undertaken with great enthusiasm

dismal – gloomy; depressing

eulogy – speech given at a funeral to honor the person who has died

jailhouse lawyer – prisoner who advises fellow inmates on legal problems

longevity – span of life

Nobel Prize – prestigious award given once a year to outstanding
individuals in several areas, including medicine, science, and literature

pervaded – spread throughout

recant – to contradict; to deny that one has made a statement

rooming house – place which provides food and a room for a fee

segregated – to separate or set apart from others

theology – the study of religion and the nature of God

*James Earl Ray was a
"jailhouse lawyer"*

*"Segregated" water
fountain*

TIMELINE

1929 *January 15:* Martin Luther King Jr. born

King graduates from seminary school

1948 *February 25:* King becomes Baptist minister

1951

1953 *June 18:* King marries Coretta Scott

1955

1956 Montgomery Bus Boycott ends

1958 *September 20:* King stabbed by Izola Curry

December 1:
Rosa Parks refuses to surrender her seat on city bus

December 5:
Montgomery Bus Boycott begins

1963

1967

1968

August 28:
King delivers "I Have a Dream" speech

April 23:
James Earl Ray escapes from prison

November 27:
King announces plans for Poor People's Campaign

King's birthday becomes federal holiday

1983

February 12:
Black sanitation workers strike in Memphis

April 4:
King assassinated

June 8:
James Earl Ray arrested

INDEX (*Boldface* page numbers indicate illustrations.)

PHOTO CREDITS

Cover, Martin Luther King Center; 1, Flip Schulke Archives; 2, Charles Moore/Black Star; 3, UPI/Bettmann; 4, The Bettmann Archive; 5, Martin Luther King Center; 6, 7, 8, 9, UPI/Bettmann; 10, 11, AP/Wide World Photos; 12, Flip Schulke Archives; 13 (top), UPI/Bettmann; 13 (bottom), 14 (top), AP/Wide World Photos; 14 (bottom), UPI/Bettmann; 15, Flip Schulke/Black Star; 16, 17, 18, AP/Wide World Photos; 19, Flip Schulke/Black Star; 20, AP/Wide World Photos; 21 (top), UPI/Bettmann; 21 (bottom), Flip Schulke/Black Star; 22, UPI/Bettmann; 23, Archive Photos; 24, UPI/Bettmann; 26, Dan Loftin/Black Star; 27, AP/Wide World Photos; 28, Flip Schulke/Black Star; 29, Martin Luther King Center; 30 (top), UPI/Bettmann; 30 (bottom), The Bettmann Archive; 31 (top left and middle left), Martin Luther King Center; 31 (bottom left), AP/Wide World Photos; 31 (right), UPI/Bettmann

ABOUT THE AUTHOR

R. Conrad Stein was born and raised in Chicago. He has published more than eighty books for young readers, including many titles in the Cornerstones of Freedom series. He lives in Chicago with his wife and their daughter, Janna.

When Martin Luther King Jr. was murdered, Mr. Stein was a social worker on Chicago's West Side. He saw some of the rioting firsthand. Most of all he remembers the mood of the nation in the days after the assassination—how shocked and deeply saddened many Americans felt about this terrible crime.